Bush Theatre

T0347027

THE ARRIVAL

by Bijan Sheibani

21 November 2019 – 18 January 2020
Bush Theatre, London

THE ARRIVAL

by Bijan Sheibani

Cast

Tom	**Scott Karim**
Samad	**Irfan Shamji**

Creative Team

Playwright and Director	**Bijan Sheibani**
Set and Costume Designer	**Samal Blak**
Lighting Designer	**Oliver Fenwick**
Sound Designer	**Gareth Fry**
Movement Director	**Aline David**
Costume Supervisor	**Rebecca Jayne Rawlinson**
Casting Director	**Amy Ball CDG**
Production Manager	**Marco Savo**
Stage Manager	**Rike Berg**
Assistant Stage Manager	**Hanne Schulpé**

CAST

Scott Karim | Tom

Scott trained at Royal Academy of Dramatic Art.

Theatre credits include: *Oklahoma!* and *The Country Wife* (Chichester Festival Theatre); *The Village* (Theatre Royal Stratford East); *Young Marx* (Bridge Theatre); *Food* (Finborough Theatre); *Imogen* and *The Merchant of Venice* (Shakespeare's Globe); *King Lear* (Royal & Derngate and ATG); *Brave New World* (Royal & Derngate and Touring Consortium); *The Invisible* (Bush Theatre); *Dara, Great Britain* and *Othello* (National Theatre); *Ladybird* (Secret/Heart); *Cymbeline, The Brothers Karamazov, The House of Special Purpose, Romeo and Juliet, All for Love/Marriage a la Mode, The Tempest, Ajax, Undiscovered Country* and *The House of Ramon Iglesias* (RADA); *Masked* (RADA Director's Showcase).

Television credits include: *The Dumping Ground* and *Holby City* (BBC); *Dracula* (Hartswood Films); *Crazy Diamond 'Electric Dreams: The World of Philip K.Dick'* (Leftbank for Channel 4 & Sony Television); *Britannia* (Amazon/Sky).

Film credits include: *White Girl.*

Irfan Shamji | Samad

Irfan was born in Zambia, attended RADA and graduated in 2017.

In his final year of RADA, Irfan played Laertes in Kenneth Branagh's production of *Hamlet*, opposite Tom Hiddleston.

Other theatre credits include: *Hedda Tesman* (Chichester Festival Theatre); *Mayfly* (Orange Tree Theatre); *One For Sorrow* (Royal Court) and *Dance Nation* (Almeida Theatre).

He was the recipient of the Clarence Derwent Award for his performances in *Mayfly, One For Sorrow* and *Dance Nation.*

Television credits include: *Urban Myths* and *Informer* (BBC).

Film credits include: *Red Joan* and *Murder on the Orient Express.*

Irfan recently voiced characters for Netflix's *Dark Crystal: Age of Resistance*, produced with the Jim Henson Company.

CREATIVES

Bijan Sheibani | Playwright and Director
Bijan Sheibani is a freelance theatre, opera and film director.

Most recent theatre credits include: *The Brothers Size* (Young Vic); *Dance Nation* (Almeida Theatre); *Barber Shop Chronicles* (National Theatre) and *Circle Mirror Transformation* (Home Manchester). In 2018 *Barber Shop Chronicles* toured to full houses in Australia and New Zealand after two sell-out runs at the National Theatre in 2017. It toured the USA for four months in 2018 and is currently touring the UK. It went to the Roundhouse in London for six weeks last summer.

Bijan also directed the UK tour of his National Theatre production of *A Taste of Honey* by Shelagh Delaney.

Recent opera credits include: *Nothing for Glyndebourne* (Danish National Opera) which was nominated for a 2017 Southbank Sky Arts Award for Best New Opera, and *Tell Me The Truth About Love* (Streetwise Opera)

Bijan has directed two short films, *Groove is in the Heart* and *Samira's Party*, both of which were selected for the BFI London Film Festival and other international festivals.

In 2019 he will direct *Morning Song* for Film Four, which he has also written It is produced by Camilla Bray and Nathanael Baring.

He was an associate director of the National Theatre from 2010–2015 under Nicholas Hytner and Nick Starr and artistic director of ATC from 2007–2010. He won the James Menzies-Kitchen Award for Young Directors in 2003 and held the John S Cohen Bursary at the National Theatre Studio from 2003–2004. He was nominated for an Olivier Award in 2010 for Best Director for his production of *Our Class*, and his production of *Gone Too Far!* by Bola Agbaje won an Olivier Award for Outstanding Achievement in an Affiliate Theatre in 2008. *The Brothers Size* won Best International Production at the Barcelona Critics' Circle Awards 2008 and was nominated for an Olivier Award in the same year. Bijan's production of *Nothing* for Glyndebourne was nominated for a 2017 Southbank Sky Arts Award for Best Opera.

Samal Black | Set and Costume Designer
Born in the Faroe Islands, Samal graduated in Design for Performance from Central Saint Martins London, and won the 2009 Linbury Prize for Stage Design. Samal's work was chosen to represent the UK as part of the Make/Believe: UK Design for Performance 2011–2015 exhibition at the V&A, previously at the Prague Quadrennial.

Productions include: *Don Giovanni*, *The Marriage of Figaro*, *Carmen* and *Così fan tutte* (Teatro dell'Opera di Roma); *Hamlet* (Gothenburg Opera); *Paria* (Teatr Wielki, Poland); *Dance Nation* (Almeida Theatre); *Circle Mirror Transformation* (HOME, Manchester); *Khovanshchina* (Winner – Best New Production, International Opera Awards 2015); *Otello* (nominated for the 2010 RPS Music Award for Opera and Music Theatre); *Life is a Dream*

(Birmingham Opera Company); *Falstaff* and *Fidelio* (Bucharest National Opera); *Anthropocene* and *The Devil Inside* (nominated for Outstanding Achievement in Opera at the UK Theatre Awards 2016); *In the Locked Room* and *Ghost Patrol* (Winner –South Bank Sky Arts Award for Opera 2013), (Scottish Opera); *Svadba* (Festival d'Aix-en-Provence); *Les Mamelles De Tiresias* (De Nationale Opera Amsterdam, La Monnaie Brussels, Aldeburgh Music, Juilliard Opera, Festival d'Aix-en-Provence); *Tosca* (Opera Ostfold, Norway); *Eugen Onegin* (Theater an der Wien in der Kammeroper); *Giasone*, *Agrippina*, *Simon Boccanegra*, *The Siege of Calais*, *L'incoronazione Di Poppea* (English Touring Opera); *Tell Me the Truth About Love* (Streetwise Opera); *Havfrúgvin* (National Theatre of the Faroe Islands); *Macbeth* (Geurilla Theatre, Seoul); *How to be an Other Woman* (Gate Theatre); *The Madman's Garden* (Kultuurikatel Tallinn, Estonia); *Y Tŵr* (Music Theatre Wales).

In 2007 he was awarded the Thorvald Poulsen av Steinum Award.

Oliver Fenwick | Lighting Designer
Theatre credits include: *Julius Caesar*, *The Drunks*, *The Grain Store* (RSC); *The Contingency Plan* (Bush Theatre); *Mary Stewart* (Hipp Theatre, Sweden); *Hedda Gabler* (Gate Theatre Dublin); *Happy Now?* (Cottesloe NT); *Private Lives*, *The Giant*, *Glass Eels* and *Comfort Me with Apples* (Hampstead Theatre); *Endgame* (Everyman Liverpool); *Far from the Madding Crowd* (ETT tour); *The Lady from the Sea*, *She Stoops To Conquer* and *On the Piste* (Birmingham Rep); *The Elephant Man* (Lyceum Sheffield and tour); *Kean* (Apollo Theatre, West End); *Jack and the Beanstalk* (Barbican Theatre); *Pure Gold* (Soho Theatre); *Henry V*, *Mirandolina* and *A Conversation* (Royal Exchange Theatre, Manchester); *Terms of Endearment* (tour); *Restoration* (Bristol Old Vic and tour for Headlong); *My Fair Lady* (Cameron Mackintosh/National Theatre tour production); *The Caretaker* (Tricycle Theatre); *The Comedy of Errors*, *Bird Calls* and *Iphigenia* (Crucible Theatre, Sheffield); *The Doll's House* (West Yorkshire Playhouse); *Sunshine on Leith* (Dundee Rep and tour); *Heartbreak House* (Watford Palace Theatre); *A Model Girl* (Greenwich Theatre); *The Solid Gold Cadillac* (Garrick Theatre, West End); *The Secret Rapture* (Lyric Shaftesbury Avenue); *Noises Off*, *All My Sons*, *Dr. Faustus* (Liverpool Playhouse); *The Chairs* (Gate Theatre); *Follies*, *Insignificance* and *Breaking the Code* (Theatre Royal, Northampton); *Tartuffe*, *The Gentleman from Olmedo*, *The Venetian Twins*, *Hobson's Choice*, *Dancing at Lughnasa*, *Love in a Maze* (Watermill Theatre); *Fields of Gold* and *Villette* (Stephen Joseph Theatre); *Cinderella* (Bristol Old Vic); *Hysteria* and *Children of a Lesser God* (Salisbury Playhouse).

Opera credits include: *Samson et Delilah*, *Lohengrin* (Royal Opera House); *The Trojan Trilogy* and *The Nose* (Linbury ROH); *The Gentle Giant* (The Clore ROH); *The Threepenny Opera* (for the Opera Group); *L'Opera Seria* (Batignano Festival).

Gareth Fry | Sound Designer

Gareth trained at the Central School of Speech & Drama in theatre design.

Recent work includes: *Harry Potter and the Cursed Child* (London, New York, Melbourne, San Francisco, Hamburg); *The Encounter* (Complicité); *The Barber Shop Chronicles*, *Draw Me Close* (National Theatre); *Still No Idea* (Improbable); *Invisible Cities* (MIF).

Other work includes: *The Master and Margarita*, *Shun-kin*, *Endgame* (Complicité); *Black Watch* (NT Scotland); CBeebies *Thumbelina*, *The Snow Queen* (BBC); *The Secret Agent* (Theatre O); *The Noise* (Unlimited); *The Cherry Orchard*, *Wild Swans*, *Hamlet* (Young Vic); *Othello*, *The Cat in the Hat*, Kneehigh's *A Matter of Life and Death*, *Attempts on Her Life*, *Waves* (National Theatre, England); *Victory Condition*, *B*, *Road* (Royal Court); *Othello* (Frantic Assembly); *John* (DV8, National Theatre).

He is the author of *Sound Design for the Stage*.

Awards include an Olivier Award, Tony Award, Drama Desk Award, and Outer Critics Circle Award for *Harry Potter and the Cursed Child*; a Special Tony Award, Drama Desk Award, Helpmann Award and an Evening Standard Award for *The Encounter* (with co-designer Pete Malkin); an Olivier Award and Helpmann Award for *Black Watch*; an Olivier Award for *Waves*; and an IRNE Award for *Wild Swans*.

Aline David | Movement Director

Aline's theatre credits include: *A Taste of Honey*, *Barber Shop Chronicles*, *Romeo and Juliet*, *Emil and the Detectives*, *Damned by Despair*, *Antigone*, *The Kitchen*, *Greenland* and *Our Class* (National Theatre); *Macbeth* and *The Merchant of Venice* (RSC); *Dance Nation* and *The House of Bernarda Alba* (Almeida Theatre); *The Brothers Size*, *Dutchman*, *Eurydice*, *Elektra*, *Parallel Macbeth*, *The Invisible Woman* and *Playsize* (Young Vic); *The Iphigenia Quartet* and *How to be An Other Woman* (Gate Theatre); *The Tempest* (National Youth Theatre); *First Love is the Revolution* (Soho Theatre); *Romeo and Juliet*, *A Taste of Honey* and *Alice* (Sheffield Crucible); *Of Mice and Men* (Birmingham Rep); *Looking for Yogurt* (Birmingham Studio); *Antony and Cleopatra*, *Much Ado About Nothing*, *Troilus and Cressida* and *Handel and the First Messiah* (Shakespeare's Globe); *Proof* (Menier Chocolate Factory); *Waiting for Godot* (West Yorkshire Playhouse); *Dead Heavy Fantastic* (Liverpool Everyman); *Gone Too Far!* and *Wanderlust* (Royal Court); *1984*, *Macbeth* and *The Mighty Waltzer* (Royal Exchange Theatre, Manchester); *A Christmas Carol* (Sherman, Cardiff); *Tarantula in Petrol Blue* (Aldeburgh, Snape Maltings Concert Hall); *The Owl and the Pussycat* (Royal Opera House Olympic Project); *Working* (Royal Academy of Music); *Nothing* (Glyndebourne Opera/Den Jyske Opera); and *Daphne* (La Monnaie, Belgium).

Amy Ball CDG | Casting Director

Recent theatre includes: *Glass. Kill. Bluebeard. Imp*, *the end of history...*, *ear for eye* and *The Children* (Royal Court); *Girls and Boys*, *Escaped Alone* and *Cyprus Avenue* (Royal Court/NY); *The Ferryman* and *Hangmen* (Royal Court/West End/NY); *Sweat* and *Berberian Sound Studio* (Donmar Warehouse); *Stories*, *Exit the King*, *Consent* and *Our Ladies of Perpetual Succour* (National Theatre); *The Hunt*, *Shipwreck*, *Dance Nation* and *Albion* (Almeida Theatre); *The Son* (Kiln Theatre/West End); *Night of the Iguana*, *Rosmersholm*, *True West*, *The Birthday Party* and *Who's Afraid of Virginia Woolf?* (West End); *The Brothers Size* (Young Vic) and *A Very Very Very Dark Matter* (Bridge Theatre).

THANK YOU

Bella Dartura-Clare and Nevio Dartura

Michael J. Leopold

Nina Steiger

The Arrival was developed with the support of the National Theatre.

Bush
Theatre

Bush Theatre, 7 Uxbridge Road, London W12 8LJ
Box Office: 020 8743 5050 | Administration: 020 8743 3584
Email: info@bushtheatre.co.uk
bushtheatre.co.uk

Alternative Theatre Company Ltd
The Bush Theatre is a Registered Charity and a company limited by guarantee.
Registered in England no. 1221968 Charity no. 270080

Bush Theatre

We make theatre for London. Now.

The Bush is a world-famous home for new plays and an internationally renowned champion of playwrights. We discover, nurture and produce the best new writers from the widest range of backgrounds from our home in a distinctive corner of west London.

Recent successes include Arinzé Kene's *Misty*, which transferred to the West End and *Jellyfish*, Ben Weatherill's love story about a young woman with Down's Syndrome which transferred to the National Theatre and a re-imagining of Jackie Kay's 1986 masterpiece, *Chiaroscuro*, directed by the theatre's Artistic Director Lynette Linton.

We are excited by exceptional new voices, stories and perspectives – particularly those with contemporary bite which reflect the vibrancy of British culture now.

Located in the newly renovated old library on Uxbridge Road in the heart of Shepherd's Bush, the theatre houses two performance spaces, a rehearsal room and the lively Library Bar.

 Supported by
ARTS COUNCIL
ENGLAND
 h&f
hammersmith & fulham

bushtheatre.co.uk

THANK YOU

The Bush Theatre would like to thank all its supporters whose valuable contributions have helped us to create a platform for our future and to promote the highest quality new writing, develop the next generation of creative talent, lead innovative community engagement work and champion diversity.

PUBLIC FUNDING

If you are interested in finding out how to be involved, please visit **bushtheatre.co.uk/support-us** or email **eleanortindall@bushtheatre.co.uk** or call **020 8743 3584.**

THE ARRIVAL

Bijan Sheibani

Acknowledgements

Special thanks to the following people without whom this play would not exist:

Meriel Sheibani-Clare, Francesca Raphael-Lincoln, Marian Sheibani, Mehdi Sheibani, Jion Sheibani, George Sheibani, Dora Sheibani, Benjamin Parker, Aline David, Samal Blak, Scott Karim, Irfan Shamji, Nina Steiger, Rebecca Lenkiewicz, Simon Stephens, Jack Bradley, Clare Slater, Lynette Linton, Deirdre O'Halloran, Jessica Campbell and the team at the Bush Theatre.

B.S.

4

Characters

SAMAD, *male. Half-Iranian. Around thirty*
TOM, *male. Half-Iranian. Around thirty-five*

Notes

Beats are around a second long.

Pauses are two to three seconds long.

Long pauses are four to five seconds long.

Silences are longer.

/ is an interruption mark.

[Brackets] like these mean the word or phrase is thought but
not said.

*This text went to press before the end of rehearsals and so may
differ slightly from the play as performed.*

1.

TOM *and* SAMAD *are mesmerised.*

TOM. Where are you in your photo?

SAMAD. Which photo?

TOM. On your profile page?

SAMAD. Oh that. That's erm… yeah, that's actually in erm… the Bayou, near New Orleans?

TOM. Oh right… I could see you're on a boat so…

SAMAD. Yeah, it was erm, this er, day trip I did when I was over there?

TOM. Oh right.

SAMAD. I was there about a year ago?

TOM. On holiday?

SAMAD. No for work?

Beat.

There were like crocodiles and stuff.

TOM. Really?

SAMAD. Yeah, it was er… amazing.

Beat.

You're in computers?

TOM. Yeah. I run my own business so…

SAMAD. I saw that. Wow. How long have you been doing that?

TOM. Four years, coming up for four years?

SAMAD. Uh-huh.

Beat.

TOM. You're in publishing…

SAMAD. Yeah the company I worked for recently folded, but erm, normally, yeah…

TOM. Uh-huh.

Beat.

What was that other photo? There was another one on there of some enormous fly that had landed on your shoe?

SAMAD. Oh yeah… there was this er… bug… so I took a picture.

TOM. What was it?

SAMAD. Erm… a kind of dragonfly I think? I'm not sure really.

Beat.

And is it a gig you're at in your one?

TOM. Yeah it's a festival I was at last summer. I went with some friends from school.

SAMAD. Oh I think I saw them in the photo.

TOM. Yeah, that's Mark and Jonny, they were just down for the weekend…

SAMAD. Right.

Beat.

Where was the gig?

TOM. O2.

SAMAD. Right.

Beat.

I've not been there.

TOM. It's alright.

Beat.

So what happened?

SAMAD. When?

TOM. With your leg?

SAMAD. Oh. Twisted it. Pulled a ligament.

TOM. How?

SAMAD. Surfing?

TOM. Ouch.

SAMAD. I mean I don't normally surf. It was a friend's stag do. And then I was walking around on it that evening, thinking it was okay…

TOM. Yeah.

SAMAD. And then it blew up.

TOM. Ooo.

SAMAD. I mean it's alright now.

TOM. Is it?

SAMAD. But at the time…

TOM. Yeah.

SAMAD. It was agony.

Beat.

It sort of came out of nowhere. One minute I was up on the board, you know, high as a kite…

TOM. Yeah.

SAMAD. And the next…

SAMAD *makes a quick weird sound and gesture.*

TOM. Mmm.

Pause.

SAMAD. And they say ligaments don't really heal properly so…

Beat.

TOM. You didn't tear it did you?

SAMAD. No no they said I pulled it.

TOM. Well, I think if you'd torn it, that would be pretty bad but
    / since…

SAMAD. No, it was a pull, I pulled it.

TOM. You'll probably be okay then… I pulled a ligament and it
    took about two months to heal so it'll probably be the same
    for you.

    Beat.

    Genetically I mean.

SAMAD. Oh right yeah course… yeah.

    Pause.

TOM. Have they given you some exercises to do?

SAMAD. Exercises?

TOM. Physio?

SAMAD. No.

TOM. You need to get onto your GP. Get some physio.
    Otherwise it won't heal properly.

SAMAD. Oh right.

TOM. You don't want it to heal stretched.

SAMAD. Stretched?

TOM. Your ligament's like a cable? There's lots of little strands,
    and when you pull it, you're basically tearing lots of those
    little strands?

SAMAD. Uh-huh.

TOM. And if the ligament heals in a stretched way, it will mean
    that the joint can move in ways it's not meant to, because the
    ligament is too loose? And that will be painful, and cause
    you all sorts of problems.

SAMAD. Oh shit.

TOM. So you just need to get some physio.

SAMAD. Okay.

TOM. I know someone. If you need it. But you should be able to get it through your GP for free.

SAMAD. I'll call them yeah thanks.

Beat.

What happened with you?

TOM. Huh?

SAMAD. You said your ligament had also…

TOM. Oh. A crash.

SAMAD. Oh right.

TOM. It was a race, so. And I crashed.

SAMAD. Oh no.

TOM. Strictly speaking I got crashed into.

SAMAD. Oh God. What sort of race?

TOM. Ironman?

SAMAD. Ironman?

TOM. Two-and-a-half-mile swim, hundred-and-twelve-mile bike ride, and then a marathon?

SAMAD. All in one day?

TOM. Yeah.

SAMAD. That's amazing.

TOM. It was fucking soul-destroying. I came off on the last hill.

SAMAD. Oh I just meant…

TOM. It's okay. I did another one. Year after. You get back up.

SAMAD. I can't imagine.

TOM. It's just a pain barrier. That's what you've gotta think. You reach it, and every time you do it hurts a bit less. You break through it.

Beat.

It'll be the same for you. We're likely to have the same thresholds.

Pause.

I couldn't believe it in her letter when she said where you live.

SAMAD. I know. What are the chances?

TOM. I know. Out of the whole of London, whole world... you move here.

SAMAD. I know. We probably like / passed each other on the

TOM. Passed each other on the street...

SAMAD. Yeah.

TOM. And didn't even realise.

SAMAD. Amazing.

TOM. It is, right?

SAMAD. Course.

Beat.

We were all so happy. Relieved to know that you were okay.

Beat.

TOM. I've spent so much of my life wondering... passing people on the street... and now, yeah...

SAMAD. Yeah...

TOM. You're here.

Blackout.

2.

A bar. Loud music.

SAMAD. I've been telling everyone about us...

TOM. Have you?

SAMAD. Meeting... Yeah, people keep asking to see your photos, asking all sorts of things about you... things I don't even know the answers to yet! It's intense. I feel like a celebrity!

TOM. Ha.

SAMAD. You know, I actually went to your apartment block like three years ago?

TOM. Did you?

SAMAD. There was this girl I was sort of seeing, and she lived there.

TOM. What was her name?

SAMAD. Christine?

TOM. Christine... doesn't ring any bells.

SAMAD. Well I came there one night, so when I found out where you lived, I was like I've been there! I know those flats! It was so weird.

TOM. Wait Christine? Christine from my apartment block?

SAMAD. Yeah.

TOM. You're kidding me?

SAMAD. What?

TOM. I went out with Christine!

SAMAD. What? What the fuck? When? / What?!

TOM. Joking joking.

SAMAD. Ugh!

TOM. Ugh! That would be like incest.

SAMAD. My God!

TOM. Ha ha.

SAMAD. Fucking hell fucking hell you got me…

TOM. I got you.

SAMAD. You totally got me.

TOM. Ha. I don't know her. Sorry.

Pause.

SAMAD. That was funny.

A lull.

TOM. Your mum said you just split up with someone.

SAMAD. What?

TOM. Your mum said you just split up with someone!

SAMAD. Oh right.

TOM. Just in passing you know.

SAMAD. What, in an email?

TOM. Yeah. We've not spoken. Just yeah, just in an email.
She was asking me about Maya… and how long we've been
together and I was telling her all about that and then yeah,
I just asked about you.

SAMAD. Oh right.

Beat.

TOM. She said you'd done the splitting.

SAMAD. Yeah, no I erm… ended it, yeah. She said I love you…

TOM. Right.

SAMAD. And I just thought that's it.

TOM. Uh-huh.

SAMAD. We weren't living together exactly but like all her
stuff was at mine, so yeah, she said it, and I obviously didn't

say it back, but we never talked about that, it was just the beginning of the end for me... you know?

TOM. I see.

Beat.

SAMAD. And...

SAMAD *laughs.*

TOM. What?

SAMAD. No I... no it's just... there was erm... I dunno...

TOM. What?

SAMAD. Nothing it's just she started to have this... this... smell... not a bad smell... it was just this smell... this metallic kind of smell... coming off her skin... like copper or something... and... it just... I don't know... I just felt like... it kind of started to... make me feel... repelled? Even though it wasn't a bad smell? Have you ever...

TOM. Erm...

SAMAD. Sorry I know it's weird... I would just go in to kiss her and it would just hit me and repel me, and it definitely wasn't there at the beginning, as far as I could tell, and then I started to think that maybe we're actually... like we as people... are actually like drawn to how people smell... or something... I dunno.

Pause.

TOM *laughs slightly through his nose.*

SAMAD *looks at him.*

A weird moment.

TOM. Sorry I was just thinking about this friend of mine who – (*Clears throat.*) made me laugh this week.

SAMAD. Oh yeah?

TOM. Yeah he said we should try and make some money. Pff!

SAMAD. Ha.

TOM. You and me.

SAMAD. Oh yeah?

TOM. Yeah. Yeah.

> *Beat.*

> Cuz – (*Swallows and laughs.*) he reckons there'll be some scientists somewhere looking into nature and nurture… and yeah… this is pretty [unusual]… you know?…

SAMAD. Yeah… it is!

TOM. To meet…

SAMAD. To meet…

TOM. A full…

SAMAD. A full… yeah.

TOM. You know… [sibling]

SAMAD. Yeah.

> *Beat.*

TOM. Cuz you did English didn't you?

SAMAD. Yeah.

TOM. Well you see I did maths.

SAMAD. Sick.

TOM. I was more into maths. So!

> *Weird pause.*

SAMAD. I was good at maths.

TOM. Yeah?

SAMAD. Yeah. Yeah I was really good.

TOM. Oh right. Cool.

> *Beat.*

> What A levels did you do?

SAMAD. English, maths and Latin.

TOM. Latin?

SAMAD. Yeah.

TOM. Oh right. Did you go to a private school then?

SAMAD. Yeah.

TOM. Oh right.

SAMAD. Yeah. I mean we didn't pay, it was erm… one of those erm… [assisted places]

Beat.

They've got rid of them now… but erm the government used to pay for you to go to a private school if your income was low. So er Mum got me to take these tests, and er… yeah. I got in.

Pause.

TOM. Did Yasmin go there as well then?

SAMAD. Yeah.

TOM. Oh right. Cool.

Beat.

What was that like then?

SAMAD. Erm, it was okay. It wasn't like an amazing school or anything.

TOM. But it got you both into Cambridge.

SAMAD. Huh?

TOM (*louder*). I said it got you both into Cambridge.

SAMAD. Yeah.

Pause.

What about you?

TOM. What?

SAMAD. What sort of school did you go to?

TOM. Just a normal one. Just the local comp.

SAMAD. Right. And how was that… was that…

TOM. Pretty shit.

SAMAD. Right.

Pause.

TOM. I mean it wasn't shit. It got me into Leeds. It wasn't like a failing school, it was just…

Pause.

It was just the school at the end of our road, you know?

SAMAD. Yeah.

Blackout.

3.

An Iranian restaurant. Iranian music.

TOM. Scandinavia.

SAMAD. Oh.

TOM. Yeah.

SAMAD. Oh right. That's interesting.

TOM. Yeah. They're not really into the heat, so…

SAMAD. Uh-huh…

TOM. Hence Scandinavia.

SAMAD. So what was it just a city break or something?

TOM. No, a cruise.

SAMAD. Oh wow!

TOM. A four-week Baltic Leisure cruise. With their church.

SAMAD. Oh okay.

TOM. My idea of a nightmare. A tour of churches, and a lot of birdwatching. My dad's into birds.

Beat.

The heat's not really for them. They've got very pale skin?

SAMAD. Oh right.

TOM. A lot paler than yours and mine so…

SAMAD *laughs*.

Pause.

What's 'ko-resht'?

SAMAD. Oh yeah, it's a kind of stew?

TOM. Ko-resht.

SAMAD. Yeah. *Kho*resht.

TOM. *Kho*resht?

SAMAD. Yeah khe.

TOM. Khe.

SAMAD. Khe.

TOM. Khe.

SAMAD. Yeah that was it.

TOM. Khe. Khe.

SAMAD. Yeah!

Pause.

TOM. Did your dad cook this stuff a lot then?

SAMAD. No no, not at all, no no, Mum just picked it up when his relatives came to stay, so...

TOM. Oh right. D'you speak Farsi then?

SAMAD. No! No I wish... no... Dad talked to me a little bit in it when I was really young, but he stopped? I think Mum was just always asking him what you saying now what you saying now so yeah...! I tried to learn it again a few years ago, but...

TOM. Uh-huh.

SAMAD. Yeah...

Beat.

I'd like to learn it though.

TOM. Yeah.

SAMAD. Hey maybe we could learn it together!

TOM. Yeah.

Pause.

SAMAD. And are your [parents]... Are they okay with you, you know... [getting in touch]?

TOM. Yeah, yeah, yeah, yeah I told them, you know, it's going really well... and that you're being so... (*Laughing.*) welcoming...

SAMAD *laughs.*

My sister had... she'd done this a while ago, and yeah, well... that didn't go so well. So... I didn't wanna put them through all that again.

SAMAD. Sure.

Beat.

TOM. I mean I'd had the birth certificate for a while, you know, with their names...

SAMAD. Yeah.

TOM. But I'd never really had any… I dunno… curiosity…
    you know… any desire… to get in touch…

SAMAD. Right.

   Pause.

TOM. But I dunno… one day… I dunno…

   Beat.

   One day my fingers were just typing it in.

SAMAD. What without you even…

TOM. Yeah.

SAMAD. Wow.

TOM. Yeah.

   Beat.

   And I was suddenly on her website.

   Beat.

   Some sort of home dressmaking thing?

SAMAD. Yeah.

TOM. And I clicked 'about me'. Read they were still together.
    Suddenly had this picture, you know?

SAMAD. Yeah.

TOM. Of the four of you.

   Pause.

   I was surprised to see that they were still together to be honest.

SAMAD. Yeah?

TOM. Yeah.

SAMAD. Why?

TOM. Er, because it's not… well it's not that common.

SAMAD. Isn't it?

TOM. Usually it's a one-night stand.

SAMAD. Right.

TOM. Or you know... a rape...

Beat.

But that they were still together and had two children...

SAMAD. Yeah.

TOM. That was... yeah... that was a surprise.

Pause.

SAMAD. And have you always known you were... [adopted]?

TOM. Yeah. Yeah, yeah, yeah, no I've always, my parents erm, my parents erm, they had this erm, they gave me this... book...

SAMAD. Right...

TOM. When I was little...

Beat.

So I've always known.

Beat.

And I've always felt you know... I dunno... different...

SAMAD. Different?

TOM. Yeah you know... as I was growing up... compared to my friends... I've always felt like I had all these questions... I mean... for example this bit of hair... I thought you'd all have this bit of white hair that I've got right here, but you erm...

SAMAD. No.

TOM. You...

SAMAD. No.

TOM. You erm...

SAMAD. No.

TOM. Don't.

Beat.

What about you? How long have you known?

SAMAD. Erm… a few years.

TOM. A few years?

SAMAD. Yeah. Five years… six years…

TOM. Oh right.

Beat.

Is that all?

SAMAD (*trying to keep things light*). Yeah… no it erm… yeah we didn't know until… it sort of all came out you know in a sort of erm family erm…

TOM. Argument?

SAMAD. Yeah.

Kind of.

Weird pause.

I mean it wasn't an argument… it was more of a… it was a bit of a weird time… she erm… Mum was going through this weird…

Beat.

(*Lightly closing it down.*) Yeah she's erm struggled sometimes in that way.

TOM. Right.

Pause.

Must have been a. Shock.

SAMAD. Yeah.

Sort of.

Beat.

Not exactly. But yeah.

Beat.

TOM. It wasn't a shock?

SAMAD. It kind of… I dunno… it kind of weirdly made sense of things.

TOM. Sense of things? What things?

SAMAD. Things that weren't talked about…

TOM. Like what?

Beat.

SAMAD. Like erm… photos that didn't exist?

TOM. Like what?

SAMAD. Like erm… photos of their wedding day.

TOM. Oh. Oh right.

SAMAD. But I never wondered where those photos were.

Long pause.

TOM. Why aren't there photos of their wedding day?

SAMAD. Oh because they did it very quickly… cuz she was pregnant?

TOM. Oh. With me?

SAMAD. Yeah.

TOM. Oh. Oh I see…

Long pause.

Were they thinking of keeping me then?

SAMAD. I don't know… I don't know when they decided to…

Long pause.

Blackout.

4.

TOM*'s flat.*

TOM. They took your bike?

SAMAD. Yep. And my bag, with my keys. Dev's away so I couldn't even get into my flat.

SAMAD kind of stumbles.

TOM. Are you okay?

SAMAD. Yeah yeah no yeah I'm fine.

Beat.

He's back tomorrow, so…

TOM. Whatever, stay as long as you like.

Beat.

Have you cancelled your bank cards?

SAMAD. They took my phone.

TOM gets his phone out, puts in his passcode and gives it to SAMAD. SAMAD searches the internet for the correct phone number.

TOM. Haven't you got your job interview tomorrow?

SAMAD. Yeah.

SAMAD puts the phone to his ear.

Can I borrow a tie?

TOM. Yeah.

Pause.

Hey. It's midnight.

SAMAD. Yeah. Sorry.

TOM. Happy birthday.

SAMAD. Oh yeah. Cheers.

Blackout.

5.

A street.

TOM. Think you got it?

SAMAD. No. I dunno. Maybe? Yes? I have no idea. I was the youngest by about ten years, so fuck knows.

TOM. Oh well. This'll cheer you up.

SAMAD. What?

TOM. Till your insurance comes through.

SAMAD. Oh... wow... but... what are you gonna do?

TOM. I'm gonna get another one.

Beat.

SAMAD. Are you sure?

TOM. Yeah but it's a one-and-a-half-grand bike so you're gonna need two locks not just the one... and I'd rather you didn't leave it outside unless you have to, to be honest...

SAMAD. No sure sure I'll be careful with it.

TOM. Happy birthday.

SAMAD. Thanks.

TOM. We can go for a ride this Sunday if you like depending on your [leg].

SAMAD. Yeah, no I think I can cycle, it's a different / group of muscles and ligaments.

TOM. It's a different group of muscles and ligaments.

Pause.

So! Yasmin!

SAMAD. Yeah...

TOM. I thought there was something you weren't telling me!

SAMAD. I know. She needed to be the one to / [tell you]

TOM. Her second!

SAMAD. Yeah!

TOM. And they're still so young! Was it planned or…?

SAMAD. Oh. I think so… yeah… I don't actually know to be honest… but it didn't seem to be an accident from what she'd said.

TOM. Right.

Beat.

Boy or girl?

SAMAD. It's too early to know…

TOM. Oh yeah. Course.

Beat.

Your parents must be pleased.

SAMAD. Yeah. Yeah, yeah, yeah, yeah, yeah… yeah. They're thrilled.

Beat.

TOM. Hey I was thinking…

SAMAD. Uh-huh…

TOM. I know you haven't got much money right now, but I've got some air miles…

SAMAD. Oh right…

TOM. And I thought we could go over there. Together.

SAMAD. Oh yeah?

TOM. To see her. In Berlin. I could book us some tickets.

SAMAD. Oh yeah. Great!

TOM. 'The uncles come to visit!'

SAMAD. Yeah!

TOM. From what she's been saying she's got plenty of room. Everyone's got more room out there haven't they?

SAMAD. No no they have…

Beat.

TOM. How was last weekend?

SAMAD. Oh yeah! Fine fine yeah I wasn't there for long, just went for the Saturday night but erm, yeah they're looking forward to tomorrow… to meeting you…!

TOM. Are they?

SAMAD. Yeah course!

TOM. Yeah.

Beat.

We've been emailing quite a bit so.

SAMAD. Yeah.

TOM. Did she say?

SAMAD. Yeah.

TOM. Okay. Sending pictures and…

SAMAD. Yeah.

TOM. Yeah. Did she show you them?

SAMAD. Yeah.

TOM. What. All of them?

SAMAD. Erm… I dunno. There were quite a lot, so… Maybe?

TOM. Okay. What and all the messages?

SAMAD. No. Not all of them. No, they're between you and her. No course not she just read some things out.

TOM. Right. What?

SAMAD. Erm… God, I can't remember now. Just the bit about how you didn't necessarily expect to hear back.

TOM. Oh.

SAMAD. She liked that bit.

TOM. Oh. Why?

SAMAD. Showed sensitivity she thought.

TOM. Oh right.

Long pause.

SAMAD. And what erm… when are you… you just going for the day right?

TOM. Yeah, yeah she said erm, to come for the night, / but erm…

SAMAD. Oh.

TOM. Yeah thought I'd just go for the afternoon.

SAMAD. Yeah, no that makes sense.

TOM. Yeah.

Beat.

Probably would have been put in your old room!

SAMAD. Yeah!

TOM (*laughing*). Which would have been a bit weird!

SAMAD (*laughing*). No, sure! Yeah!

Beat.

I mean none of my stuff's in there now.

TOM. No, but still.

Beat.

SAMAD. And there's a spare room. It was Yasmin's room.

Beat.

Well they're both spare now.

Pause.

TOM. And the train's pretty easy isn't it?

SAMAD. Yeah. No yeah it is.

TOM. Waterloo right?

SAMAD. Yeah, yeah it's really easy from there. / Direct so.

TOM. Two hours right?

SAMAD. Yeah.

TOM. And you can walk right from the station?

SAMAD. Yeah.

TOM. Yeah I could see on erm… on the… Google Maps, it's a nine-minute walk, so…

SAMAD. They can pick you up I'm sure.

TOM. Oh yeah, well.

SAMAD. I mean they'll probably want to.

TOM. Mmm.

SAMAD. They will want to I mean. Obviously.

Beat.

TOM. Do they drink?

SAMAD. Yeah they drink.

TOM. Okay… I just thought maybe… your dad didn't drink.

SAMAD. Oh, no, he's not religious.

TOM. No? He's not Muslim?

SAMAD. I mean he was, when he was a kid… but not now…

TOM. Hasn't stuck your mum in a burka, got her reciting the Koran?

SAMAD *laughs politely.*

SAMAD. No.

Beat.

TOM. There's a new wine shop actually, it's just opened up on the high street. So yeah think I'll get something from in there. They drink wine?

SAMAD. Yeah they drink wine. I'm sure whatever you bring you know… it'll be… appreciated.

TOM. Yeah.

Beat.

SAMAD. They'll just be really looking forward to meeting you.

TOM. Yeah.

SAMAD. I mean they are. They told me. So…

TOM. Did they?

SAMAD. Yeah.

Blackout.

6.

Cycle trip. Countryside.

TOM *eats.*

TOM. Funny.

SAMAD. Funny?

TOM. Yeah he's just funny.

SAMAD. Funny how?

TOM. Just, dunno, just made me laugh.

SAMAD. Funny ha-ha or…?

TOM. Yeah. Yeah he's funny. I guess I didn't expect him to be so eccentric.

SAMAD. Eccentric?

TOM. Yeah. Idiosyncratic. You know? He's quite a joker. A practical joker. Not like my dad at all.

SAMAD. No?

TOM. No. Not at all. My dad's quite serious really. I don't wanna say immature cuz he's not.

SAMAD. Who?

TOM. Your dad.

SAMAD. Oh.

TOM. But there's something… juvenile isn't there? He was sort of doing this funny dance in the kitchen when your mum was putting the lunch out.

SAMAD. Oh, right, yeah.

TOM. I mean it was funny. But just a bit. Juvenile.

SAMAD. He looks young for his age I guess. He does a lot of running. Like you.

TOM. Yeah no we talked about that, about his running.

SAMAD. Yeah.

TOM. But it wasn't that. It wasn't the way he looked. It was something else. Can't quite put my finger on it.

Pause.

SAMAD *starts coughing.*

You okay?

SAMAD. Yeah, no, that last hill just took it out of me a bit.

Pause.

TOM. He's been going for quite a few years right.

SAMAD. Running? Yeah.

TOM. Must be genetic.

SAMAD. Yeah.

TOM. Runner's build.

SAMAD. Yeah.

TOM. I said to your dad next time I come I'll run with him.
Bring my stuff. Run along the beach. Nice place to run.

SAMAD. Yeah.

TOM. You should start.

SAMAD. Maybe.

TOM. Then you could come too.

Beat.

Some of his stories though.

SAMAD. What?

TOM. They're hard to follow.

SAMAD. Really?

TOM. Yeah he was telling me one about a repair job he was
on… some electrical emergency involving a wasps' nest?

SAMAD. Oh yeah.

TOM. But he kept missing bits out, so I had to keep asking him
who do you mean now?

SAMAD. Yeah, no well, he gets nervous, he was probably
nervous, you know, so…

TOM. Yeah. Yeah maybe.

Beat.

And he was shorter than I expected.

SAMAD. Shorter?

TOM. Yeah. I dunno, just from the photos. Because he's so thin.
He looked… well he was shorter than I expected him to be.
In my head he was tall. Like me.

Beat.

But I guess he's more your height.

SAMAD. Yeah.

TOM. Bit taller maybe?

SAMAD. Erm, yeah, I think I'm ever so slightly taller than him.

TOM. Is your mum's family tall?

SAMAD. Not particularly.

TOM. I just wondered where I got my height from.

SAMAD. I think my dad's probably shrunk a bit. You know, with age.

TOM. Right. Happens.

SAMAD. And you went to the beach.

TOM. Yeah, we went to the beach. Eventually. Took them a while to get out of the house. Your mum went in her electric chair.

SAMAD. Her scooter.

TOM. Her, yeah her electric chair. She called it her electric chair. I said to her I wouldn't mind one myself. She's quite dangerous in it, speeding along the pavement.

SAMAD. Was she?

TOM. Fifteen mile an hour. At least.

SAMAD. Yeah.

TOM. One guy had to jump out of the way.

SAMAD. Really?

TOM. I'm not joking.

Beat.

And once we got down there, she couldn't go far, cuz the battery would run out she said, and she needed to get back, so we just sat there for a bit on the prom, and then turned back.

Pause.

Bit weird going down there, without going onto the actual beach. I tried to persuade her. The wheels looked pretty sturdy to me, but she was having none of it…

Long pause. Perhaps they imagine going up to a beach but not going onto it.

And that pier you've got down there, I'd probably seen pictures, or something, but I just got this sense of... déjà vu. You know when you get that?

SAMAD. Yeah.

TOM. Weird.

Long pause.

Your mum's on a lot of meds isn't she?

SAMAD. Oh?

TOM. Yeah. She was popping them back.

SAMAD. Oh. Well she gets pain.

TOM. What a lot?

SAMAD. Well. Comes and goes.

TOM. She said she'd slept badly.

SAMAD. Yeah, no she does, when she's got pain. She has bad nights.

TOM. Thought she was gonna trip out the amount she was knocking back! I said no wonder you don't drink much!

Beat.

Didn't go down very well.

Pause.

How long's she been like that?

SAMAD. Like what?

TOM. With her leg.

SAMAD. Oh. A long time.

TOM. Oh.

SAMAD. Yeah.

Beat.

TOM. How'd it happen?

SAMAD. Nerve damage. In her back. Her spine, so…

TOM. Oh what. Broken?

SAMAD. Yeah.

TOM. How?

SAMAD. She had an accident.

TOM. What sort of accident?

SAMAD. Erm. She had a fall.

TOM. Fall?

SAMAD. Yeah.

Pause.

TOM. What sort of fall?

SAMAD. Erm, I don't know…

TOM. You don't know?

Beat.

SAMAD. I don't really know the erm details…

TOM. Haven't you asked her?

SAMAD. Erm… I don't… really… wanna… erm… I just…

Beat.

I don't really…

Beat.

I just know that it was from… something quite high up?

Long pause.

TOM. Something quite high up.

SAMAD. Well yeah.

I mean.

Long pause.

It wasn't exactly a fall.

More of a

Pause.

TOM (*realising*). Jump?

Silence; eight seconds.

When did it happen?

SAMAD. Just after I was born.

Silence; ten seconds.

She erm, they enjoyed meeting you.

TOM. Yeah?

SAMAD. Yeah. No they said that they'd had a good time.

TOM. Right.

SAMAD. Yeah. For sure.

TOM. Well that's good.

Blackout.

7.

SAMAD*'s flat.*

SAMAD *is anxious.* TOM *is pumped.*

TOM. Oh. You're not ready.

SAMAD. What time is it?

TOM. Seven.

SAMAD. Oh.

TOM. What?

SAMAD. Is that today? What day is it?

TOM. Monday.

SAMAD. Oh shit sorry.

TOM. We can start on Wednesday.

SAMAD. No, no, I've been really distracted... sorry. I'll just get ready. Sorry.

SAMAD *exits to get ready.*

TOM. I don't wanna be late.

SAMAD. I'll be two secs.

TOM. I've gotta be back by seven forty-five...

Silence. TOM *alone in running gear in his brother's flat.*

How's the fancy job?

SAMAD. Yeah. Still in shock. Nice to have some money.

TOM. I bet.

SAMAD *comes back in and does up his shoelaces.*

What's distracting you?

SAMAD. Huh?

TOM. You said you were distracted.

SAMAD. Oh. Yeah. Dev's given me notice.

TOM. What?

SAMAD. Yeah…

TOM. How come?

SAMAD. He promised the room to his mate so…

TOM. So he's just kicking you out?

SAMAD. Yep.

TOM. What you gonna do?

SAMAD. I dunno. Start looking.

Beat.

TOM. You staying in the area?

SAMAD. Maybe… it's expensive though so…

Beat.

I dunno.

Beat.

TOM. When do you have to move?

SAMAD. End of the month.

TOM. Shit…

SAMAD. Yeah…

TOM. Okay…

Beat.

Well if I hear of anything…

SAMAD. Thanks.

Pause.

TOM. Quick warm-up?

SAMAD. Okay.

TOM. Follow what I do.

About five seconds of TOM *stretching, and* SAMAD *copying him before they speak. They continue the stretching and warming up under the dialogue.*

What's your budget?

SAMAD. I'm paying six-fifty at the moment, but I could probably stretch to like eight-fifty, nine-fifty now...

TOM. You need to start saving, get a deposit together.

SAMAD. Yeah... I've got a lot of debts though so...

TOM. I've got a little bit put by... I'm looking at buying a second flat... not at the moment but in the future... could go in together if you can save enough? Good investment for me... (*With a warm-up move.*) Hah!... good incentive for you... (*And another.*) Hah! Need to get your foot on the property ladder... stop living like a student...

SAMAD. Yeah... yeah I mean... yeah.

TOM. That the T-shirt I gave you?

SAMAD. Yeah.

TOM. Fits huh?

SAMAD. Yeah.

TOM. I was saying to Maya now I've got a brother it's quite tempting to buy two of everything!

SAMAD. Ha. Yeah!

TOM. Bit lower. Yep that's better.

Beat.

Shake it out.

They shake it out. TOM *makes loud sounds as he does.*

Okay?

SAMAD. Yep.

TOM. Let's go.

They run.

You feel okay to talk?

SAMAD. What?

TOM. You should be able to maintain a conversation while running. Just let me know if it starts to feel too difficult and we can slow down.

SAMAD. Okay.

TOM. You don't wanna push things at the beginning. Slow and steady wins the race.

They keep running.

How's your leg?

SAMAD. Yeah feels good.

TOM. Just say if it starts to twinge.

SAMAD. I will.

TOM. Stay on the grass?

SAMAD. Oh yeah.

TOM. Protects you from / too much impact

SAMAD. Too much impact I know.

They run.

Pause.

TOM. Maya's got someone for you to meet.

SAMAD. Oh yeah?

TOM. Yeah. She's fit. And she's met me, so she'll know what to expect. I told her my brother's in publishing and doing a half-marathon so she wanted to meet you. She's a literary type, so you might hit it off.

SAMAD. What does she do?

TOM. Something in PR? I dunno.

Beat.

And she liked your photo.

SAMAD. My photo?

TOM. On Facebook.

SAMAD. Oh.

TOM. Hope you don't mind, she wanted to see you, so…

SAMAD. No that's cool.

Beat.

TOM. How long were you with Tina?

SAMAD. Six months.

TOM. So you split just before we met, which was just over two months ago so you'll probably be over it in about a month. Takes half the amount of time you were together to get over it apparently.

SAMAD. Uh-huh.

TOM. Quicker if you get together with someone else.

Beat.

You haven't got together with anyone else yet have you?

SAMAD. No.

TOM. No, okay. Was gonna say that would have been quick.

SAMAD. I wasn't that into it to be honest. So. I don't think I've got much to get over. I did the splitting up, so…

Running…

Did you get to your sister's on time last night?

TOM. Yeah, just about.

SAMAD. Did she have a good birthday?

TOM. Yeah think so. She was off her face, but that's how she does it.

SAMAD. A lot of people there?

TOM. Yeah, a lot of her mates from back home...

SAMAD. And your parents?

TOM. Yeah my dad gave a speech, so.

Beat.

They wanna meet you by the way.

SAMAD. Huh?

TOM. My parents.

SAMAD. Oh yeah?

TOM. Yeah. If you're up for that?

SAMAD. No no definitely.

TOM. Okay. Maybe next time they're down?

SAMAD. Great yeah.

TOM. Next weekend?

SAMAD. Wow okay.

TOM. Thought we could go to the Indian again.

SAMAD. Again?

TOM. Yeah, where we're going tonight.

SAMAD. Oh I see. Is that tonight?

TOM. Yeah. Mondays.

SAMAD. Great, yeah, it's Monday, yeah...

Beat.

Ow.

TOM. Y'okay?

SAMAD. Yeah… just a slight twinge.

TOM. Wanna stop?

SAMAD. No I'm okay. It was my other leg so.

TOM. Stop for a sec? Let me feel?

TOM *finds a knot in* SAMAD*'s calf, and massages it for a moment.*

Okay?

SAMAD. Yeah.

TOM. Stretch it out.

SAMAD *stretches it out.*

Bit lower. How's that?

SAMAD. Fine.

TOM. Think you're dehydrated. Here.

TOM *gives him water.*

Pause.

SAMAD. Nice view.

TOM. Yeah.

SAMAD *takes in the view.* TOM *doesn't.*

Look, I know it's early days, but given your situation… what would you say to moving in with me?

SAMAD. What? But what about Keith?

TOM. He's been talking about moving out for a while. I can give him a month's notice. Less if he finds somewhere else.

SAMAD. Are you serious?

TOM. I've got to cover my mortgage so I wouldn't be able to do it for six-fifty but we could say nine-fifty including bills… and given how much we're seeing of each other anyway…

SAMAD. Uh-huh.

TOM. And it'll make things a bit easier when the folks are coming to stay. Or Yasmin. When she's over in London. Kill two birds with one stone you know?

SAMAD. Yeah.

Beat.

TOM. Okay? Shall we give it another go?

SAMAD. Erm, yeah… but maybe we should erm… [head back]

TOM. First rule of a good training programme? Listen to your body. We'll head back… warm down with a nice gentle jog.

The brothers run…

8.

SAMAD. Yeah…

TOM. Yeah?

SAMAD. Yeah… yeah I mean… they're nice, they're really nice.

TOM. Yeah.

SAMAD. Yeah.

Beat.

And your dad's really interesting… he's obviously really passionate about nature. All that stuff about birds and habitat loss was…

TOM. Yeah.

SAMAD. Pretty shocking.

TOM. Mmm.

SAMAD. And was your mum okay?

TOM. What d'you mean?

SAMAD. No I just… she just seemed in a bit of a daze but
I guess / she was just

TOM. Oh… no, no, no, she's fine. It's just a bit weird for her.
She kept saying afterwards 'you're like two peas in a pod –
you're like two peas in a pod'.

Beat.

She liked you. They both did.

SAMAD. Uh-huh.

TOM. So thanks. For coming.

Beat.

I think you know, for them… it's not that easy.

SAMAD. No no I bet.

TOM. So.

SAMAD. Yeah.

Beat.

TOM. I mean obviously they're pleased, that it's going well.
And that we're moving in together.

SAMAD. Yeah.

TOM. But for them it's hard.

SAMAD. Of course.

TOM. You know because, well. For obvious reasons.

SAMAD. Yeah.

TOM. Yeah.

Beat.

I mean they wouldn't want it to have not gone well. I mean
when it didn't go well for my sister, that was… well. It was
yeah, quite horrendous. I mean that's partly because of her.

She's got you know… issues… and she sort of relapsed as a result.

SAMAD. Relapsed?

TOM. Yeah.

SAMAD. Oh right.

TOM. Yeah. She was… yeah… well… don't tell her I told you this if you meet her… but yeah, she had to have quite a lot of help. In the past. Professional help. Drugs. You know?

SAMAD. What, she was on [drugs]?

TOM. Yeah. She was doing the lot.

SAMAD. Right.

TOM. And it was exacerbated when she tried to get to know her biological mum. Her mum was an alcoholic so… it's probably genetic.

Beat.

So obviously they're really pleased, you know that it's all going so well. So. Thanks. I mean it was important that, you know for me, that they were sort of included in all of this, you know?

SAMAD. Yeah.

Beat.

TOM. So I don't know if, you know, your mum and dad would be up for it, but I know mine would be.

SAMAD. What?

TOM. Oh. Meeting. All of us.

SAMAD. Oh.

TOM. Yeah.

SAMAD. Right.

TOM. Like a sort of family reunion I guess.

TOM *laughs lightly and* SAMAD *copies.*

Pause.

SAMAD. What, when?

TOM. Er whenever. Whenever's good.

SAMAD. Erm...

TOM. What, you don't think they'll want to?

SAMAD. I dunno. I mean, it's erm... I just. I don't know.

Beat.

TOM. I mean we could all meet in Bournemouth, they could go
down to Bournemouth. They wouldn't have to come here.
I know they'd be up for that, if you think that'd... make
a difference.

Beat.

Anyway, they'd be curious. Keen to. You know?

SAMAD. Yeah. I mean it's not up to me.

TOM. No I know.

SAMAD. It's up to them.

TOM. Yeah.

SAMAD. So why don't you ask them?

TOM. Yeah, yeah I was gonna. Next time I see them. I just
thought if you thought I should, or whether you should,
or what?

Beat.

SAMAD. I kind of think you should. I mean it's for your
parents.

TOM. And yours.

SAMAD. Yeah. But mainly yours.

TOM. Is it? I mean, don't you think they'd want to?

SAMAD. I think it's complicated.

TOM. Complicated?

SAMAD. Yeah.

Beat.

I don't know. What they'd want.

Pause.

TOM. They're nice people.

SAMAD. I know they are.

TOM. They're not going to be judgemental of your parents.

SAMAD. I know.

TOM. You know I've explained. I've explained that she explained. And that I understood.

SAMAD. Yeah.

TOM. Why she did what she did. Why they did what they did.

SAMAD. Mmm.

TOM. That's all in the past. It was over thirty years ago now anyway, so…

Pause.

They're not gonna be judging, you know? They just want to meet her. They want to meet both of them. You know?

SAMAD. Yeah.

TOM. It'll be fine.

Pause.

Look, so Keith's moving out a week on Saturday, I was thinking that if you didn't want the expense of a van that you and I could just start moving stuff over in my car during the week.

SAMAD. Yeah, okay.

TOM. Okay. So shall I pop round Tuesday night?

SAMAD. Great.

Blackout.

9.

SAMAD. Sorry you know, I just... there's not a lot I can do.

TOM. Okay.

Beat.

SAMAD. I mean I tried. I talked to her. I talked to both of them, and they just... well they said not yet.

TOM. Okay.

Pause.

SAMAD. I mean they're happy for me, that I've met them, and you, obviously, they've no problem with / that...

TOM. Why would they have?

SAMAD. No, I know. But what I mean is, for them... you know it's complicated.

Beat.

TOM. Why?

SAMAD. Because of what they did.

Beat.

TOM. They feel guilty?

SAMAD. No. I mean I don't know.

TOM. They don't need to. They explained. I / understand.

SAMAD. Yes I know, I know they did but...

TOM. What is it then?

SAMAD. I don't know… maybe meeting up… they might not really understand what it's for, or something…

TOM. What it's for?

SAMAD. Maybe.

TOM. It's for me. For them. For these parts of my life to somehow come together. It's for them to meet my parents… to…

I dunno…

Thank them.

Beat.

SAMAD. Thank them?

TOM. Yes.

Long pause.

SAMAD. I'm trying to say that they sometimes feel intimidated /

TOM. Intimidated? My parents are not / intimidating.

SAMAD. Yes I know and I said that… but sometimes they get an idea in their heads, a decision, and it can be hard to… convince them otherwise…

Long pause.

TOM. Is it cuz of the phone call?

SAMAD. What phone call?

TOM. I made this phone call, to ask your mum about Christmas presents.

SAMAD. Did you?

TOM. She didn't say?

SAMAD. No.

TOM. Oh. Cuz I think she was pissed off.

SAMAD. Why?

TOM. Cuz it was earlier than she's used to. She emailed to say she didn't want calls at that time of the morning.

SAMAD. Oh. Did she?

TOM. Yeah. She said she wouldn't get calls like that from you at that time of the morning, so she certainly didn't expect to get them from me.

SAMAD. Oh. I didn't know that. I'm... I'm sorry she said that. That's... really harsh. She must have been in pain or something. But still... it wouldn't be / because of a...

TOM. So maybe it's because of / that?

SAMAD. No, it won't be because of that.

TOM. How d'you know?

SAMAD. I just... know.

Long pause.

TOM. They don't need to feel guilty. That's why I got in touch. To let them know I was okay. They don't need to feel bad. I had a good home.

SAMAD. I know you had a good home, we know you had a good home, that's not the point. For years they've been wondering about where you are and suddenly you're just here and it's a lot for them to deal with...

TOM. Deal with?

SAMAD. I mean, you coming into their lives, right now, they're in a weird...

TOM. Why?

SAMAD. Place. It just is. It's a lot for everyone to get used to. It's a lot for me to get used to. And Yasmin.

Beat.

TOM. Okay. Well. I thought we were getting on.

SAMAD. We are. Of course we are. I just... I'm not used to it that's all.

TOM. Used to what?

SAMAD. Having an older brother. I'm used to being the older brother. And now you're here, telling me what to do.

TOM. I'm not telling you what to do.

SAMAD. You are! You're telling me what to say to my mum and dad!

TOM. I'm not. I was just asking you to see if they would be up for meeting my parents.

SAMAD. Okay.

Beat.

TOM. That's all.

Beat.

SAMAD. Well I did, okay?

TOM. Fine.

Beat.

SAMAD. I'm sorry, I know how important it is to you, but it's not up to me.

TOM. I know.

SAMAD. It'll happen I'm sure at some point, so. Just have to wait.

TOM. Okay.

Pause.

SAMAD. And look, I've been thinking. I know you're not gonna like this…

TOM. What?

SAMAD. And I'm sorry. But I've been thinking again. About moving in. I don't think it's a good idea.

TOM. What?

SAMAD. I think things are working well the way they are.
I think… I don't wanna put too much pressure on it all.
It's early days.

Beat.

TOM. Where you gonna go?

SAMAD. To my mate's in Clapham.

TOM. Clapham? That's fucking miles away.

Beat.

Are you stressed?

SAMAD. No.

TOM. You're busy at work?

SAMAD. No.

TOM. Just take a bit longer, wait till you can think straight.

SAMAD. I am thinking straight. It's nothing to do with work.
I don't wanna move in. I've been thinking about it a lot and
I've spoken to my parents about it, and they think that there
might be times, and I think they're right about this…

TOM. Uh-huh…

SAMAD. when I, you know, feel like occasionally that I might
want to, you know, see my sister on my own for example,
when she's over, sometimes, or them, just to have the option.

TOM. You can.

SAMAD. Yeah but if she's staying at our flat it's not so easy is
it, d'you know what I mean, or if they're just coming up for
the day then /…

TOM. Then what? I can go out, I don't have to be here, I do
have a life you know? I have my own parents. They don't
have to fucking endure me if they don't want to.

SAMAD. It's not about that.

TOM. Fucking hell.

SAMAD. What?

TOM. Why are you telling me this now?

SAMAD. What?

TOM. It's too late.

SAMAD. I'm sorry, I just think we need to have our separate space.

TOM. I've given Keith notice I'm gonna lose one thousand two hundred a month from next week.

SAMAD. I'm sorry.

TOM. You think I'm fucking made of money?

SAMAD. No.

TOM. I didn't take a deposit because I trusted you.

SAMAD. I can give you some money... I...

TOM. You've totally fucked me over.

SAMAD. Fucked you over?

TOM. Yes. You've all just decided without, without consulting me and now I've gotta deal with this shit. It's fucking out of order.

Blackout.

10.

SAMAD. Sorry I'm late, I was stuck in a meeting.

TOM. It's been ages.

SAMAD. I know. A few months right?

TOM. Six.

SAMAD. That long?

TOM. Yeah. I mean I know you said we should slow things down, but…

SAMAD. Well you were away for a month of it and then I was so…

TOM. Yeah. Yeah. How are things?

SAMAD. Good. Yeah. Really good actually.

TOM. Yeah?

SAMAD. Yeah.

TOM. Missed you last weekend.

SAMAD. I know… I'm sorry. Sophie's brother was here, so I had to meet him, and since the promotion I've been all over the place, so…

TOM. Yeah, no of course.

SAMAD. Did you have a good party?

TOM. Yeah, yeah it was alright. The rain stayed away, so…

SAMAD. Yeah?

TOM. Yeah.

Beat.

SAMAD. Well that's great. Happy birthday by the way.

TOM. Cheers.

SAMAD. I got you a present but I left it at home. I'm sorry.

TOM. That's okay.

SAMAD. Next time I see you.

TOM. Yeah.

Beat.

So what's new?

SAMAD. Well. Erm… I've got some news actually.

TOM. Yeah?

SAMAD. I'm getting married.

TOM. What?

SAMAD. Yeah.

TOM. How come?

SAMAD. What, what d'you mean?

TOM. But that was… to erm… to thingy?

SAMAD. Yeah.

TOM. The blonde one in the short skirt at that barbecue?

SAMAD. Sophie.

TOM. Yeah. Gosh.

SAMAD. Yeah.

TOM. Yeah. Wow. I only met her once.

SAMAD. Yeah.

TOM. Thought she was just a fling.

Pause.

SAMAD. I mean I know it hasn't been very long, but I've seen enough people to know, and we get on, so…

TOM. Yeah.

SAMAD. And we're in love.

TOM. Yeah.

SAMAD. So I just did it.

TOM. Right.

SAMAD. I mean I didn't even plan it.

TOM. Right.

SAMAD. I just did it.

TOM. Right.

SAMAD. And she said yes.

TOM. Right. That's amazing.

SAMAD. Yeah.

TOM. So… yeah. Wow.

SAMAD. Thanks.

TOM. What's the er… when's the… er, day?

SAMAD. Last Saturday in August I think, we just thought let's just do it, and get on with it you know?

TOM. Yeah.

Pause.

And like how did you know?

SAMAD. Know?

TOM. That she's the one, that you wanna, you know, spend the rest of your life with?

SAMAD. Erm… oh… I just know.

TOM. Yeah?

SAMAD. Yeah. Yeah, I just feel it.

TOM. Feel it?

SAMAD. Yeah. We just click.

Beat.

TOM. Have you felt that before?

SAMAD. Erm… yeah. Kind of. Yeah. But I dunno. This feels…
better.

Beat.

TOM. I don't think I've ever… I'm not sure that… I'm just not
sure I've ever felt that.

SAMAD. Oh. What about…

TOM. We split up.

SAMAD. Oh. Did you?

TOM. Yeah.

SAMAD. Oh my God, I'm so sorry to hear that.

TOM. No, no, it's fine. It was me. I wanted to. It was over
a while ago.

SAMAD. Oh I'm sorry… I've not really been in touch.

TOM. It's cool.

SAMAD. I thought she was moving in after I…

TOM. She did, and then, yeah.

Beat.

I feel better anyway.

SAMAD. Yeah?

TOM. I mean you know, I was getting home and just hoping
that she wasn't there.

SAMAD. Oh.

TOM. Yeah it was getting like that.

SAMAD. Right.

TOM. Yeah, I felt, you know kinda suffocated.

SAMAD. Right.

TOM. Yeah, like, relieved when she wasn't in. Freer. I could
move, you know?

SAMAD. Yeah.

Beat.

TOM. And she started talking about kids.

SAMAD. Oh right.

TOM. So. Yeah.

SAMAD. Mmm.

Silence.

Sorry I should have asked.

TOM. No, no why should you have known.

SAMAD. I should have asked you.

TOM. No, no, don't be silly, why should you? You've been busy.

Beat.

You've got a wedding to organise.

Beat.

Who's the best man?

SAMAD. Jimmy.

TOM. Jimmy?

SAMAD. You know, Jimmy.

TOM. Jimmy?

SAMAD. Yeah.

TOM. *Jimmy* Jimmy?

SAMAD. Yeah.

TOM. He's your best man?

SAMAD. Yeah.

TOM. Oh.

SAMAD. What?

TOM. I just, I'm surprised.

SAMAD. Why?

TOM. I didn't realise that, I didn't realise that you and he were… close.

SAMAD. Yeah. He's… yeah.

TOM. Okay.

SAMAD. Yeah.

TOM. Sorry I just. I don't think I've met him more than once.

SAMAD. Well. I've known him since I was eleven. So.

TOM. Yeah, no sure, I mean. Great.

Beat.

So what's the plan?

SAMAD. With what?

TOM. You not doing any kind of…

SAMAD. Yeah. No yeah. Yeah no I am.

TOM. Yeah.

SAMAD. I just haven't quite decided when yet.

TOM. Right.

SAMAD. Obviously you'll get an invite from Jimmy.

TOM. Yeah.

SAMAD. Yeah.

Pause.

TOM. I always imagined somewhere like Barcelona would be good.

SAMAD. Yeah. Yeah I think we're sticking closer to home.

TOM. Oh right.

Beat.

What like Newquay.

SAMAD. Erm. Probably more like London.

TOM. Oh right.

Beat.

Who's going then?

SAMAD. Ted, Detsky, Rez...

TOM (*very quietly*). Uh-huh...

SAMAD. Max, Jimmy obviously...

TOM (*very quietly*). Obviously.

SAMAD. Matt, Jon...

TOM (*very quietly*). Uh-huh...

SAMAD. Josh, Dick, Garech...

TOM (*very quietly*). Yeah...

SAMAD. Phi, Nev. I think Nev...

TOM. Why might he not be?

SAMAD. Erm, not sure if he can.

TOM. Thought you said you didn't have a date.

SAMAD. I think Jimmy might have sent round an email with some prospective dates.

TOM. Right.

SAMAD. I take it you didn't get it.

TOM. No I didn't.

SAMAD. Right. Well I'll check with him.

Beat.

TOM. Great.

Blackout.

11.

Street in the village.

SAMAD. Oh, hi.

TOM. Hi.

SAMAD. What's that?

TOM. Oh just an accident I had.

SAMAD. Jesus. What happened?

TOM. Got hit.

SAMAD. By what?

TOM. Car.

SAMAD. Fucking hell. When?

TOM. Yesterday.

SAMAD. Were you wearing a helmet?

TOM. Uh-uh.

SAMAD. Why not?

TOM. Just had my hair cut?

SAMAD. You wanna get that seen to.

TOM. No, it's just a cut. You should have seen the car.

Beat.

SAMAD. There's a doctor in the village, you could go
    tomorrow.

TOM. It looks worse than it is.

Beat.

SAMAD. You found somewhere to park then?

TOM. Yeah eventually. Your instructions weren't very good
    though.

SAMAD. Oh.

TOM. You said turn right after the pub.

SAMAD. It's left.

TOM. Yeah I know that now.

SAMAD. I wouldn't have said right.

TOM. You said right.

SAMAD. Okay.

TOM. Anyway I found it eventually.

Beat.

Traffic coming down was terrible, took me six hours, I left mid-afternoon thinking I'd get here in time for the dinner but...

SAMAD. Have you found where you're staying?

TOM. Yeah bumped into Jimmy and the stags... they said they might be still serving food at one of the pubs?

SAMAD. Oh, yeah, probably, though I wouldn't think they would be, it's after nine now, so...

TOM. Do you know which one?

SAMAD. No, sorry.

TOM. Okay.

Beat.

Where you gonna be?

SAMAD. Jimmy and I are just going to the pub...

TOM. Uh-huh?

SAMAD. But that's to go through stuff before tomorrow...

TOM. Oh right okay. Well I'll just see what the rest of them are doing. Try and find them.

SAMAD. Yeah, good idea.

Beat.

TOM. So is there anything I need to know?

SAMAD. About what?

TOM. About tomorrow?

SAMAD. No.

TOM. I don't need to do anything?

SAMAD. No.

TOM. Okay. I'm just wearing a normal tie, didn't know if there was any kind of…

SAMAD. No, there's not.

TOM. Dress code or anything.

SAMAD. No, not for erm, no.

Beat.

You know what time it starts?

TOM. Yeah, yeah I got that on the… email…

Beat.

So are you actually getting married in the marquee?

SAMAD. We're renewing the vows, we're doing the actual marrying bit before.

TOM. Oh right okay.

SAMAD. Yeah we couldn't actually get married in the marquee, so we're doing it just before in this small ceremony-room place.

Beat.

TOM. So I'll just come to the marquee?

SAMAD. Yeah.

TOM. Okay.

Beat.

So I guess I'll be meeting a lot of the family tomorrow.

SAMAD. Yeah, guess so.

TOM. Yeah. Big day.

   Beat.

   Blackout.

12.

Music.

SAMAD *and* TOM *put on their suits for* SAMAD*'s wedding.*

Later SAMAD *is wearing a ring. He looks at it.*

13.

TOM *has gone somewhere alone. He is feeling low. He is not expecting anyone to come this way.*

In the distance, music can be heard from the wedding.

He genuinely tries to express warmth towards SAMAD.

SAMAD. Hey.

TOM (*hiding his face*). Oh. Hey.

   Beat.

SAMAD. You… everything okay?

TOM. Yeah, yeah, just… came out for a bit of air. Bit of a walk.

SAMAD. Okay.

TOM. Mmm.

> *Pause.*

> (*Tenderly, with pleasure*.) He's very cute.

SAMAD. Who?

TOM. Yasmin's boy.

SAMAD. Yeah yeah he is.

TOM. Saw him dancing.

SAMAD. Yeah.

TOM. How old is he now two?

SAMAD. Erm. Two and a half?

TOM. He looks like me. Like I did.

SAMAD. Yeah.

> *Pause.*

TOM (*still trying to communicate warmly to* SAMAD).
I wanted to talk to him but erm…

> *Long pause.*

> TOM *stares at* SAMAD. *He's struggling.*

SAMAD. It's the ceilidh in a minute so…

TOM. Yeah… I'll be in in a minute. I'm a bit pissed, so…

SAMAD. Okay, yeah, no sure take your time.

> *Pause.*

TOM. That girl Shania she's a fucking prick-tease. She single?

SAMAD. Er… no. Well I don't know. She's erm, she's Moira's
friend… I can…

TOM. Where's she from, she Indian?

SAMAD. No, she's erm, think her dad's Jamaican?

TOM. Yeah, she's erm… she's nice. Fit.

SAMAD. Mmm.

TOM. There's quite a lot of fitness here, didn't expect that.

SAMAD. Mmm.

Pause.

I'd better go back in then.

TOM. Yep.

SAMAD. Come and join the ceilidh.

TOM. Yep.

Blackout.

14.

Late in the evening.

The dance floor at the wedding.

TOM *dances drunk, chaotic. Wild. Messy.* SAMAD *notices him but at first he doesn't interact very much.*

Soon TOM *is swaying, and* SAMAD *is trying to stop him from falling.*

It turns into something strange and psychological…

TOM *and* SAMAD *embracing… having fun… then a very quick flash of* TOM*'s hands around* SAMAD*'s neck… intense and determined…*

Then TOM *and* SAMAD *dance jokingly again… then another quick flash of* TOM *on his knees with* SAMAD*'s arm around* TOM*'s neck, trying to crush him…*

Then jovial again…

And then…

15.

A street in the village just outside the venue.

TOM. I'm sorry.

SAMAD. It's fine.

TOM. I'm just a bit…

SAMAD. Yeah, it's fine we'll clear it up.

TOM. Oh God I'm bleeding.

SAMAD. Let me see?

TOM. There.

SAMAD. It's okay, it's just a little cut from the glass. Here.

> SAMAD *puts a napkin on* TOM*'s hand.*

TOM. Oh fuck I've got it on your / suit, fuck.

SAMAD. It's fine, just, oh fuck.

TOM. Here let me…

SAMAD. I'm fine.

TOM. Here you can use this.

SAMAD. I'm fine.

> TOM *steps back.* SAMAD *tries to wipe the blood off himself.* TOM *watches for a second.*

TOM. Who is he anyway is he a mate? Coming round the corner at a hundred fucking miles an hour. Is he a relative of mine?

> *Pause.*

> TOM *goes to go back in.*

> I just need to go back / and talk to

SAMAD. No no no, don't go back in.

TOM. I just need to talk to him. I need to talk to him.

SAMAD. No, no, no let's just get you back to yours.

TOM. What you doing? Get off. What you doing?

SAMAD. Nothing what d'you mean?

TOM. Are you chucking me out of your wedding?

SAMAD. No of course not, Jesus, it's just late and people are going. Let's just get you back okay?

TOM. What cuz your mum told you to?

Beat.

What?

SAMAD. What?

TOM. I heard her.

SAMAD. What?

TOM. 'What?' Fucking bitch.

SAMAD. Don't talk about her / like that.

TOM. Take him home… / take him back home fucking bitch.

SAMAD. She didn't say that.

TOM. I heard her.

SAMAD. You're drunk / you're imagining things.

TOM. Get him out of here.

SAMAD. She didn't say that / that's not what she said she said why don't you help him home.

TOM. Yes she fucking did! Get him out of here. She said it.

Beat.

Why wasn't I on the top table?

Beat.

Why wasn't I? Your sister's boyfriend and Sophie's sister's boyfriend were up there.

SAMAD. Look I'll walk you back and / …

TOM. Why wasn't I in the photos?

SAMAD. What photos? You were in photos, there's loads of photos.

TOM. I was watching you all having them all taken. I have photos of you having photos, look, where's my phone, where's my fucking phone / oh fuck.

SAMAD. You are in a lot of the photos I just wanted / some without you okay?

TOM. Where's my fucking phone I need to go back in and…

SAMAD. No…

SAMAD *goes to stop him.*

Beat.

TOM. I've been nice to you haven't I?

Beat.

I've been nice to her haven't I? Why couldn't you just let me be part of things?

SAMAD. You have been part of things.

TOM. You could have warned me. It's fucking humiliating.

SAMAD. Warned you what?

TOM. That I was gonna be sitting with all your mates, and not with the people I know.

SAMAD. You can't be sitting up there with us.

TOM. Why not? Why not?

SAMAD. Because I don't want you sitting up there with everyone looking at you like some prodigal son okay? It's my day not yours. It's about me. And that's my family. It's mine.

TOM. It's also my fucking family mate. Sorry to inconvenience you, but you're my family too matey. See this, see this? It's fucking blood mate. It's all over your fucking suit okay? It's in your fucking veins.

TOM *pushes him.*

SAMAD. Don't push me.

SAMAD *pushes him back.*

Something messy and physical starts. It doesn't turn into a proper fight. During the struggle:

TOM. You're all such fucking liars. You all come across as being so fucking nice but you're just a load of fucking hypocrites.

Once they're separated...

Fuck off.

SAMAD *doesn't move.*

Just fuck off. All of you. I can walk myself home.

SAMAD *doesn't move. In the distance from the wedding we can hear a song about someone leaving someone...*

TOM *sniggers at the irony of it... is joyous at the irony of it.*

He begins to join in with the song... singing it like a football song, euphoric, the best karaoke act ever... forgetting some if not most of the lyrics... maybe he takes his shirt off...

SAMAD *exits, leaving* TOM *alone.*

The volume of the music increases until it surrounds TOM.

TOM*'s euphoria tips over into intense sadness.*

And he cries and cries and cries...

He crumbles to the ground.

And becomes foetal.

16.

A street near TOM*'s flat.*

For the first part of the scene SAMAD *might actually believe that he's with his father.*

TOM. Samad?

SAMAD. Yeah? Oh my God!

TOM. Hey.

SAMAD. Jesus Christ!

TOM. Er, Tom'll do.

SAMAD. Pff.

  Beat.

  I didn't know you were still round here.

TOM. Yeah, yeah.

SAMAD. Oh right, I heard you were erm living in Leeds.

TOM. Er, no that was ages ago. And temporary. Three years ago.

SAMAD. Huh.

TOM. Yeah.

  Beat.

  So…

SAMAD. So… you look well. Look like you've been away.

TOM. Yeah.

SAMAD. Uh-huh.

  Beat.

  Where?

TOM. Southeast Asia.

SAMAD. Oh yeah?

  Beat.

  Did you go for long?

TOM. Eighteen months.

SAMAD. Oh right. Cool.

Beat.

Holiday?

TOM. Yeah… I guess.

Pause.

What you doing round here?

SAMAD. Er, just got a meeting. Erm. My boss lives here.

TOM. Oh right.

SAMAD. Yeah. He's having a kind of late-summer-party thing at his house, so…

Beat.

What about you you just off out or…

TOM. Yeah just going out for some lunch, meeting a couple of friends.

SAMAD. Uh-huh.

TOM. Meena and Alex?

SAMAD. Oh yeah.

TOM. You remember them?

SAMAD. Yeah.

Pause.

TOM. Work going well?

SAMAD. Yeah. Yeah.

TOM. Uh-huh.

Beat.

SAMAD. What about you?

TOM. Er, bits here and there.

Beat.

You got two kids now?

SAMAD. Yeah.

TOM. What's the second?

SAMAD. A girl.

TOM. Uh-huh. How old is she?

SAMAD. She's two.

TOM. Uh-huh. So what Eddie must be five?

SAMAD. Yeah five.

TOM. Mmm.

Pause.

You stopping there or…

SAMAD. Yeah no two's enough. Sophie wants to get back to work, and erm, no two feels plenty.

Pause.

TOM. Yasmin okay?

SAMAD. Yeah. She's good. She's er fine.

Pause.

TOM. I thought you er, were trying to avoid me then.

SAMAD. What? When?

TOM. Just before.

SAMAD. No.

TOM. No?

SAMAD. No.

TOM. Okay. It just looked like you saw me, and then turned away.

SAMAD. No. I thought I er, I thought I recognised someone.

TOM. You did.

SAMAD. No, I mean… erm over there, that's why I, why it probably looked as though I was turning away. But yeah, anyway. I didn't see you so…

Beat.

TOM. Y'mum okay?

Beat.

SAMAD. Yeah. Yeah she's fine, yeah. Haven't seen her for a bit, but erm…

TOM. How come?

SAMAD. Oh, erm… I dunno… just… it's been busy you know, and I think she's been busy?

TOM. Really?

SAMAD. Yeah, erm, I think just, I probably haven't… I dunno… just…

TOM. Would have thought she'd be up here all the time given the grandchildren.

Pause.

How's your dad?

Pause.

SAMAD. Erm… he's erm… he died.

TOM. Oh.

SAMAD. Yeah. Sorry. I thought. I just… thought because of Facebook you'd have…

TOM. I stopped all that.

SAMAD. Oh right… well… sorry. I thought you'd have just found out somehow.

Long pause.

Over the remaining dialogue, TOM *very gradually realises that the father that has now died and the brother standing in front of him were a kind of fantasy…*

It's funny seeing you. I thought for a moment back there that you were him that you were my dad.

You looked like him.

You know?

SAMAD *cries.*

I thought you were a ghost.

SAMAD *cries. Through the crying:*

Sorry.

I'm so sorry.

TOM. What was it?

SAMAD. It was quick. It was his heart. It was all very sudden. He didn't… he didn't. He wasn't in any pain.

You know?

Sorry.

TOM. No I'm sorry.

SAMAD (*still crying*). Sorry we didn't tell you.

TOM. No no it's okay.

SAMAD. I just thought you'd find out, or… I dunno…

Long pause.

TOM. When was it?

SAMAD. Erm… nearly two years ago.

TOM. Right.

SAMAD. So not that recent, but it just… hits you sometimes you know?

Pause.

You look just like him. Oh my God you look so like him. So much more than I do.

Pause.

I'm sorry to just… for you to be just…

TOM. No, no, I'm erm, I'm just taking it in.

SAMAD. Are you okay?

TOM. Yeah.

Pause.

I'm sorry for your loss.

Pause.

You know?

Long pause.

SAMAD *looks at* TOM.

SAMAD. Thanks.

Pause.

I'm so sorry you know. For everything. I just…

TOM. How's your mum managing on her own?

SAMAD. Erm. Okay. She gets help. I go down when I can. We're still trying to figure all that out.

Pause.

Your parents okay?

TOM. Yeah. Yeah they're well.

Beat.

SAMAD. And you, are you okay?

TOM. Yeah yeah I'm okay. Erm. Yeah. Got a date. Tonight. So. New avenue. We've been chatting online for a while.

SAMAD. Yeah.

Pause.

TOM. I'm sorry, you know, if I did anything wrong / I just…

SAMAD. You didn't. Course you didn't. It was just… difficult you know.

TOM. I guess I just thought I'd found you guys now…

Pause.

But I hadn't.

Pause.

Well I dunno. If you're up this way… maybe I'll…

SAMAD. Yeah.

TOM. I dunno bump into you again or something.

SAMAD. Yeah.

Silence.

I was looking at my son the other day. He's just started back at school. I just… I was in the playground, and I was just looking at his little body, and I was just thinking about him being in the world, all these other children, him navigating his way through it all, and I just felt so… worried for him. He's so precious to me you know and I just wanted to be with him all the time just to make sure he's okay.

SAMAD *cries.*

It was just this little body… you know? Just this little body… and I could just feel him moving away from me you know?

D'you know what I mean?

TOM.

SAMAD. I don't know why I'm telling you this.

TOM.

SAMAD. I just wanted to be like right next to him, so that I could just whisper in his ear just anything that might make him feel better. If anything, even just something small, made him worry, that I could just take that away from him. I just don't want him to have... I don't want to... I don't want him to feel alone... you know?

D'you know what I mean?

Pause.

TOM. Yeah. I know what you mean.

The sounds of a nearby school playground... children on lunchbreak...

The sounds increase in volume until the children are all around the brothers.

They stand like that for some time.

Fade on the brothers.

Just the sound of children playing.

Then off.

End of Play.

A Nick Hern Book

The Arrival first published in Great Britain as a paperback original in 2019 by
Nick Hern Books Limited, The Glasshouse, 49a Goldhawk Road, London W12 8QP,
in association with the Bush Theatre, London

The Arrival copyright © 2019 Bijan Sheibani

Bijan Sheibani has asserted his right to be identified as the author of this work

Cover design by Studio Doug; photography by Bronwen Sharp

Designed and typeset by Nick Hern Books, London
Printed in Great Britain by Mimeo Ltd, Huntingdon, Cambridgeshire PE29 6XX

A CIP catalogue record for this book is available from the British Library

ISBN   978 1 84842 907 9

Woodland
CARBON
www.woodlandcarbon.co.uk
NICK HERN BOOKS
Printed on Carbon Captured paper